New

"He was six-two, about 160 pounds and he'd just flattened three low-life scum who'd been hassling me. He threw a cigarette into his mouth, poured me a tooth-mug of Thunderbird and said: 'What next beautiful?' He was all man. My heart was doing 140 bpm. In a tremulous little-girly voice which didn't sound like my own I asked: 'Martin Newell?' He pointed to one of the scumbags on the bar-room floor. 'That's him.' he said. Then he walked out of my life. I never saw him again."

Hollywood starlet, Melanie Oberstein.

New

Martin Newell

Off Licence Books
1999

Previous publications include:

I Hank Marvinned   The Greyhound Press, 1991
Under Milk Float   The Greyhound Press, 1992
The Illegible Bachelor   Festival Books, 1996
Poetic Licence   Jardine Press, 1996
Wild Man of Wivenhoe   Jardine Press, 1998
Black Shuck   Jardine Press, 1999

Sales and distribution by Heritage House
01255 870595 Http://www.heritage-house.co.uk

New
Design by Catherine Clark and James Dodds
Printed by Progressive Printing, Leigh on Sea, Essex

ISBN 185215-0785

I dedicate this book to Mr. Murphy of North Hill,
Colchester, a great dentist.

Thanks to:
Dr. Joe Allard of University of Essex for editing and advice,
Jane Olorenshaw for proofreading,
Jane Lindsey for bailing me out,
Roger LaHay, ditto.
Cherry Red Records,
Joachim Reinbold of Jarmusic
and the Independent Newspaper for making an honest woman of me.

Many of the selections herein were originally published in the pages of
The Independent from 1996 to 1999 and are reproduced with their kind permission.

Selections of the author's earlier work as a pop musician are available from:
JARMUSIC phone/fax 0049-5841-70244.
E-mail: jarmusic@t-online.de
and:
CHERRY RED RECORDS London England
Http://www.cherryred.co.uk

The Martin Newell U.K. Website is at:
Http://www.go.to/martinnewell
E-mail: cleanersvenus@yahoo.com
Big thanks to Paul Wilkinson who captains it.

Martin Newell is managed by Jane Lindsey Management & Promotion
(and has been for years) on 01227-712750.

New poems by the author appear in the pages of The Independent
several times a week. Perhaps you should think about reading it.

Contents

Philip Larkin In The Bedding Department At Mothercare:

They tuck you up your mum and dad...

Cannabis Debate

The year they made it legal
Or was it the year after?
A silence in the Commons
Except for stifled laughter
The Minister For Cannabis
Stood up to make his point
His shadow interrupted:
"Did you front-load that joint?"
Amidst the back-bench uproar
The Speaker shouted out:
"Order...or whatever...
Yeah...what was this about?
Taxation? Right I'm with you
So anyway these places
We've opened up in London
For people off their faces..."

"Thank you Madam Speaker."
The Minister grinned sweetly.
"The working party's seen them
We checked them out completely
Where was I? Yeah...these Cafés.
Extraordinary really...
The music on their speakers
You hear it much more clearly
It isn't muffled, thuddy
As in a normal venue
Did I say muffled, thuddy?
Or was it thuffled, muddy?
No. Anyway...their menu
Our working party tried it
The skunk was pretty edgy
But okay if you ride it

Whereas the Leb was heavy
Though nothing you can't handle
We all just sort of sat there
Staring at the candle..."
The Minister looked vacant
Remembering the night.
"Taxation?" someone prompted
He smiled and said: "Yeah...right."

"...and look. Is anyone going out?
Because I really fancy some chocolate..."

Elegy For A Drummer

A drumstick thrown into the air
Higher than the lighting rig
Frozen by the follow-spot
Seemingly just hanging there
And in the dark
The band stands by
The audience rows
With mouths like O's
Await a drummer, clad in black
Who'll catch the thing behind his back
Without a glance, will catch the stick
And cue the band in with a click
Don't knock it till you've seen the trick
Or stood backstage
In some strange town
And craned to see the thing to come down
Dropping like a splintered bird
Past a battered lighting stand
Out of darkness. Into hand.
Cozy died. You never heard?

Good drummers then.
What's it to us?
Essential to a band? Discuss...
And of how many bands d'you say:
"The drummer's good. I've seen him play"?
You noticed him. The bloke stood out.
A power-house?
The word's too trite
Does not explain the light and shade
Of which a decent drummer's made
Or whether he has got the look
The maze-bright eyes of rock star rats

The sparking of a tinderbox.
And timing of atomic clocks
"Was worth his weight in gaffer tape."
A roadie I once knew might say
And while obituaries are done,
Who did he play with?
Everyone.

A drumstick thrown into the air
Higher than the lighting rig
Frozen by the follow-spot
Seemingly just hanging there...

Gangsta Etiquette

At dinner with the record co.
A gentleman should not cry "Yo!"
Upon being asked to pass the salt
And if by chance he finds a fault
With rivals' braggadocio
He never says: "You fat mofo.
You diss me and I'll fuck your ho."
Instead he asks," Is that the time?
Excuse me but I'll have to go."

When having reached a small impasse
It's gauche to shout: "I'll whip yo ass."
He parries with, "Oh come now sir.
A valid point. I must demur."
He then avoids a slanging match
By saying "My Uzi's slipped its catch
And though this will seem declassé
Reluctant as I am, I may
Be forced to blow your face away."

If remonstration cuts no ice
A small incendiary device
Placed somewhere...say, inside a car
Of some ill-mannered gangsta star
Resolves the dispute in a trice
Discretion, though, is my advice
So detonate it while they serve
Your fellow diners with hors d'oeuvres.

Clone Home

They'll soon be cloning childless men
I think about this now and then
A vision of a world gone mad
Where Bob's your uncle
And your dad.
Then farther down the line your son
Till in the end, Bob's everyone.
Religions may declare it crime.
I'm sure that they'll relent, in time
When scientists complete their job,
We'll go to church and worship...Bob.

How The Pop Charts Work

Sales. Product. Unit. Happening.
Outlets. Target. Placing. Yep.
Video. Artwork. Brilliant. Airplay.
Money. C.D. Bullet. Rep.

Studio. Roadwork. Tickets. Mixing.
Session. Plugger. Drumtrack. Sweet.
Merger. Money. Exports. Publish.
Money. Peaking. Major. Beat.

A&R Man. Frontman. Side-man.
Promo. Wicked. Market. Big.
Money. Deejay. Money. Money.
Website. Kicking. Anthem. Gig.

Charlie. Money. Funky. Freebies.
Pressure. Dissing. Money. Track.
Techno. Deadzone. Radio. Money.
Money. Money. Favour. Crack.

Chartwise. Goodguys. Hi-Fis. Whitelies.
Soundman. Money. Pace. Respect.
Money. Glasto. Live-act. Whammy.
Money. Money. Money. Wrecked.

Money. Click-track. Ambient. Money.
Session. Guest-list. Stiff. Advance.
Money. Money. Soundscape. Money.
Money. Bootleg. Money. Dance.

Sexy. Money. Bangin'. Money.
Money. Hardcore. Money. Move.
Software. Money. Single. Money.
Mega. Money. Money. Groove.

Money. Bonus. Cash. Exclusive.
Money. Money. Business Course.
Money. Stateside. Money. Money.
Money. Money. Money. Force.

Money. Money. Money. Money
Money. Money. Money. Money.
Money. Money. Money. Money.
Money. Money. Money. Money.

Aaaaand remember kids:
Keep on buying what WE tell you to.

The Psychedelic Detective

I woke up in my office three decades later, with an atomic comedown and a taste like someone had been seeding clouds in my mouth.

I shimmied into a paisley shirt and some hipsters, sparked up a Players Number Six and considered the situation:

Syd and Jimi had hopped the blue bus, right? But where was the dame in the Granny Takes A Trip dress and the dayglo specs?

Somewhere down the hall I could hear the zupp zupp phhtt of some juvenile playing a backwards drum kit. The radio was making pink noise. I was hungry.

Two blocks down, at the Take'n'Babble, a walrus in a blazer soughed in a slowed-down voice: "What's yer poison, Bunky?" I ordered sky on rye. Heavy on the moonbeams, easy on the clouds, hold the horrors. To go.

What if the dame was right? Supposing a new breed of bent-brain brats had broken into the rehearsal bunkers and were fooling around with tape-loops, backward guitars and mellotrons?

Back at my office I had a visitor. She slid in through a crack in the skirting board and draped herself onto a beanbag. "Steady with yer psychic aura Toots. You're leaking ecto-plasm over my Book Of The Dead."

Her eyes were like a 14-hour technicolour happening. Which had happened. In a voice like clocks melting, she grated: "It's like this Johnny. The kids are sick of the baby-food. They wanna nix The Corporation's Tommy Tippee."

I slung her a No. 6 and spat: "What's new treasure? The Corp have got time. They'll note the brand of brain candy. Scarf up the sonics. Buy up the boys and sell it all back to the kids at twice the price."

She fell into my arms. All eight of them. A teardrop plished onto the linoleum and broke into millions of tiny crystals. Her kiss tasted of stars but her breath was like a dead planet. The Nu Psychedelia, huh?

She cooed: "D'y'ever get that sensation of déjà-vu Johnny?"
I blinked.
She cooed: "D'y'ever get that sensation of déjà-vu Johnny?"
I blinked.

The Rock Date Starter Kit

After months of hell with:
a) Boyhood genius
b) Wildman
c) Millionaire

Decided that I'd have :
a) To leave
b) Largactil
c) Tony Blair

His problem is he's:
a) Mad on football
b) Not Keith Richards
c) Static

And can't stop playing with:
a) Models
b) Sting
c) The trainset in his attic

Another major drawback is he's:
a) Moody
b) Still in detox
c) Barking mad

But old enough to:
a) Dress himself
b) Buy fireworks
c) Be my dad

The periodic tantrums:
a) Terrified me
b) Are hilarious
c) Not on vid

My only souvenir's his:
a) Bank book
b) Secret diary
c) Kid

As soon as I get:
a) Well
b) Remedial surgery
c) A good lawyer

I'm going to:
a) Marry Mick
b) Rebuild my life
c) Sell G.M. Soya

The Mark I Popstar's Girlfriend

There she is in black and white
The universal rock star's girl
A daughter of a saxon earl
All sunsilk hair and daisy-eyed
Scooped up to be the faery bride
Of some pop atheling, refugee
Who nicks her from the gallery
And barely out of County High
Or convent school, she drinks the light
Actress/model/supermuse
But having got the clothing right
Emerges fun-furred, spaced out, skinny
Sparrow-legged from purple mini
Her handbag full of boyfriend's pills
A PhD in shopping skills
She learns to sing a bit, she cooks
And fills the popstar's pad with books
Is this week's Bardot up to scratch?
"Comme un ange," calls Paris Match
Before she falls. And how she falls.
Washed up, dumped and hollow-eyed
Her boudoir littered with dead friends
And this is how the first part ends

Three decades on and back she comes
A slight rondeur, a tad more grey
But waking at her publisher's
She baked a cake, she wrote a play
She auctioned off her husband's things
The lithographs, Moroccan rings
Made albums, gave good interview
Her voice was fractured, way too blue
(Lilli Von Schtup, to me and you)

But girls today should learn from her
Those blonde bombsites we witness now.
Perhaps Mark l could teach Mark ll
To come back from decline with grace
We'd save a lot of tabloid space.

Twelve Inch Remit

When things go wrong
With your c.d.d.d.d.d.d.d.d
Re-mem-mem-mem-mem
How those vinyl records used to be
Cordsusedto be/Cordsusedtobe

With all that jumping up and down
At least the vinyl kept you fit
Nylkeptyoufit/Nylkeptyoufit
Unless you fixed the lightweight arm
With plasticine or two pee bit.

The thing about the vinyl is:
It's warm, it's big, it's analogue.
The ear interprets this, much as
A drinker will a cup of grog
Lacupofgrog/Lacupofgrog.

And record sleeves, being large,
Allow traditional activities;
The chopping, rolling, counting-out
Essential to young debauchees.
Ungdebauchees/Ungdebauchees.

And here's a vinyl thought for all
You long-play freaks to contemplate
Being born in '45 meant
You were 33 in '78
Yinseventyeight/Yinseventyeight.
Yinseventyeight/Yinseventyeight.

Railway Poem

Hi. This is your railway poem
For customers to Cardiff
I'm sorry that it cannot rhyme
Until we get to Swansea
Those who wish to hear a switch
Of metre before Newport
Should change at Bristol Parkway
Where an iambus is waiting
This is due to shortages
Of syllables in Swindon
Your poem is running
Approximately
Three feet short.
I do not yet know
Why it has stopped.

Snowbirds

It's a mad amount of money
Buys a small amount of powder
Makes the conversation louder
And the mediocre clever
From the land of never-never
Where the toilet is a palace
Comes a symphony of sniffing
It's a mad amount of money

A sheen upon the upper cheek
A beak-lunch for a busy week
My god, it's bloody boring
Watching some pathetic geek
Pat the stash-bag in his pocket
While he tries to play the star
In a fashionable khazi
Which purports to be a bar

For a dab of nuclear sherbert
It's a mad amount of money
As they disappear for ages
And the atmosphere goes funny
On the stilted paranoia
Of the insecurely groovy
With designer sinus headache
And a nostril which is runny

In the provinces, the people
Who are last along the queue
Get a little in for Christmas
For their girlfriends and themselves
Cos it makes them feel naughty
When they get to over forty

With the healthy-lifestyle leaflets
On their pastel-coloured shelves

It's a mad amount of money
For a frozen little smile
From a trollop in the papers
Whose stupidity's in style
And it's really wild and wacky
What these dazzling people do
I expect Bolivian children
In the jail cells think so too.

The Final Makeover

Death becomes the fading idol
Better than mascara could
Not all of the good die young
Often though, the young die good.

The whippet-skinny roadie, Death
Is ligging in your dressing room
Hanging round the stage and stairways
Twitchy like a virgin groom.

Dine on doom you starstruck troupers
Death the pussycat will let you
Right until the feast is over
When the fortieth brandy gets you.

Death the drummer in your backline
Only makes the beat get stronger
Vita brevis in your biog
Guarantees your ars lives longa.

Age the taxman trims your fan-base
Quit before they drift away
Death, the first and last accountant
Won't object to how you pay.

Shotgunned by a jealous lover
Cudgelled by a cult in Norway
Found with fruit and naff narcotics
Hanging from a hotel doorway.

Better dead than out-of-cred
Portly on the comeback rota
Rocking on in spite of rancour
Far more sense to roll the motor.

There beside you Death the groupie
In your Limo, horny, plastered
Immortality lies gagging.
Go on. Do it. Die ya bastard.

The Summer Of Love

According to the history books
The drug got lots of coverage
And everyone was tripping out
Except for Malcolm Muggeridge
But as a simple schoolboy
The business puzzled me
This sacrament-on-sugar-lumps
They all called LSD;
Which vengeful secretaries
Dropped in their bosses' tea
To send them off to Narnia
Psychotic as could be

And several pop aristocrats
Who'd turned their brains to mince
Made albums in the afterglow
Unequalled ever since
In all the years which followed
We've built on this romance
Though most of what they tell you
Is actually pants.

In summer 'sixty-seven
Well...where can we begin?
The buses ran as normal
The harvest was brought in
Old Labour banned the pirates
In spite of a campaign
And what we got was Radio One
And Flowers In The Rain
But no-one in my area
Drew flowers on their cheeks
As blokes with bogbrush haircuts
Might chase you round for weeks.

Unless you lived in Chelsea
Where being weird was legal
For then you whopped the acid down
And called your love-child Seagull
Spent decades in a commune
In Somerset or Devon
Until you entered Parliament
In nineteen ninety-seven.*

*Probably.

And So The God Of Easy Listening Said:

You should buy this, kids
You really should
And not just in a post-modern
Ironic sort of way
Because during the sixties
When your Dad
Was lying on a muddy greatcoat
At a three-day pop festival
Not far from Lewes
Being straddled
By a wild girl called Suzie Sunchild
Who is now called Mrs. Clarke
And probably runs a Sue Ryder Shop
Somewhere in Berkshire,
This is what his mum listened to
As she ironed his spare flares
With the hipster, three-inch belt loops
And the tapestry patches.
All the while, humming along
In her best he'll-grow-out-of-it way

Yeah you should buy this, kids
Because Andy's backing singers
In some cases here
Were those loveable
Amphetamine chipmunks,
The Osmond Brothers
In all their close harmony
Enamel-stripping former glory
No really. Do this for your Dad.
Make a cassette of Andy Williams
Send it to him and your step-mum
Wish him all the best

With his Tai Chi Workshops
Point out to him how fresh it sounds
Compared to say, Jefferson Airplane
Because his mum was right.
And he was wrong.
And we're all straight now
So it's okay to like it
Almost like a war's over.

Sooty — My Drug Hell

When the scandal broke, a tight-lipped Sooty
Baseball cap pulled down across his face
Read the papers, speeding from the courtroom
Tabloid hacks on motorbikes gave chase

Current pictures of the pale puppet
Contrast badly with an early one:
Happier days with drum kit by the sea-side.
"What Is Wrong With Sooty?" screams The Sun.

Panda Sue: "We all just felt so powerless.
Watching him descend the slippery slope
No-one knew the pressure he was under
And I guess he found it hard to cope."

In a private clinic near Roehampton
Sweep toyed with his salad and confessed:
"Me an' Soot? We went for it, yeah. Big-style.
But it's what you do when you're the best.

Don't think we're the only ones to go there.
Teletubbies. They won't last the pace.
Check out Tinky Winky on a bad day.
There's a boy who isn't on the case."

Sooty: "Everyone's been so supportive
All the cast have sent me cards and stuff
Since the story broke on Monday morning
That was when the gig got really rough.

Hopefully the worst of it's behind me
Now that Geri's brought me here to France
And of course, George Michael lent his chateau
Thanks to them I've got this second chance.

That's the danger when you're in this business
Some of us burn out before we peak
Look at Sweep, he never got his voice back
Over forty years he's had that squeak

Not something you talk about in public
Basically, you fear what fans will think
People's hands inside you each performance
That's the one that sends you to the brink."

The Winterval Manifesto

Shepherds watching flocks by night
Must cease work by 9.00 p.m.
In line with set Working Hours limits.

The cattle are lowing.
The baby awakes.
Ring our Noise Pollution Hotline

The holly and the ivy
Now they are both full-grown
Have been deemed unsuitable for use
Since the holly is not child-friendly
And the ivy may affect asthma sufferers.

Elves will report to Team Leader,
Ms. Ryan, for her keynote speech:
"Paper Chains In A Workshop Context"
A hands-on assembly instruction session
Will provide facts on a Need-To-Know basis.

Boxing Day is rescheduled for 2nd Jan. 1999
Renamed: Courtesy Visit/Gift Interface Day,
It will allow those workers in non-aligned jobs
A compensatory Comfort and Joy period.

Differently-nosed sub-arctic deer
Must not be subjected to workplace harassment
And will receive fair employment consideration
Under the Equal Opportunities Act.

Safety headgear must be worn at all times
In a one-horse open vehicle.
Laughing all the way.

Our Winterval Patriarch will visit you.
He may seek to gain entry via your chimney
We apologise if he calls at an inconvenient hour.
Under the 1994 Toy Recipients Charter,
You may be entitled to compensation.

Counting Sheep

Among those rain-green purple hills
Beneath that tableau of the clouds
The ruthless choreography
And dressage of the collie "creep"
The smartest dogs to walk the earth
Will wheel and weave, even in dreams
While city workers fall asleep
Yan, tyan, tethera, counting sheep

For here is man but here's his dog
A fur-machine with dustbin breath
As border collie owners know
They have this look, the collie eye
Reserved for nervous visitors
The children, cats or anything
The creature may identify
As necessary to bring "by".

To see the collies working though,
A symphony in monochrome
From occiput to tip of tail
Along a valley hell-for-leather
Narrow hips and galleon chests
A canny canine S.A.S.
In marinade of Cumbrian weather
Another matter altogether

Yan, tyan, tethera, methera, pimp
The farmers now go down the ramp
And head towards the shedding ring
As rural England goes for broke
And governed by remote control
Becomes a film-set, set-aside
A tale of complex country folk
Being treated as sort of joke

Lethera, hovera, dovra, dick.
The collies bring the last ewes in
And semi-telepathically
Will drive them in a pincer sweep
The smartest dogs to walk the earth
Can wheel and weave, even in dreams
While city workers fall asleep
Yan, tyan, tethera, counting sheep

Yan, tyan, tethera, methera, pimp,
sethera, lethera, hovera, dovra, dick,
are numbers 1 to 10 in old Cumbrian
dialect used for counting sheep.

The "Easy" Divorce Sketch

Her lawyers said to write it down
The muttered curse, a fleeting frown
Refusal to co-operate
If reconstrued might lend some weight
As proof in court. Effective? Rather.
Unfitness as the children's father.
The means become the end alone
And sacrificed upon that stone
All money time and sanity
To please this great god, Custody.

His lawyer. Reassuring. Posh
Did sod all good. Still took the dosh.
Not infidelity. As such.
They fought? Of course. She spent too much.
The house, the kids, the car...the lot.
His drinking. That began the rot.
"Don't shout!" Which prompted one attack.
"I've just got in...she's on me back
The kids are crying. It's hurling plates.
That's it. On sofa. Round me mate's."

Could hardly saw the house in half
Could he? Reason with her? Laugh?
Down the pub, his mates had said,
"She's got you now mate." Better dead
Than join the Sunday Father Squad.
End up some bitter, sad old sod
The kids collected from her door
One frantic weekend out of four
And shouted at, when one was sick
"I SAID not many SWEETS. You THICK?"

She for her part, knackered, lonely.
Sometimes got out. Weekends only
Men seemed slightly wary now
More fish in sea, less bites somehow.
They didn't mind that she'd been wed
They found out she'd got kids, they fled
The maintenance? Well that was late.
Her mum said, "C.S.A. You wait."
And then the bastard wriggled free.
Just killed himself. Deliberately.

Skittish Safety Standards Approved

The bold inventor left his lab
to test on this occasion
A new device for meeting friends
of similar persuasion
Discretion being the better part
of valour in such cases
He waited later in the day
to put it through its paces

But cruising through a Surrey park,
the man and his invention,
A fellow of a different stripe
and amorous intention
Approached him in the thickening gloom
fired-up by the vibration
And pointed out: "Some badgers too,
stop at the Other station.

Despite cross-species bonding
being especially taboo
That sound you make attracts me so
I'll break the rules for you
Though badger-human interface
Is frowned on by the law
Why shouldn't man and badger
step out proudly hand-in-paw?

My father would be horrified
and likely die of shock
Those Shaving Brush atrocities
still haunt the older brock
There's more to life than cubs and wife
and what our folks can't handle

Is youngsters forage far and wide
to seek what lights our candle.

Not just a case of Badger Pride
but badger courage too
And batting for the other side
I bat my eyes at you
I wouldn't say our first foray
will go without a hitch
But please don't run away from me.
Well...suit yourself, you bitch."

"Goats Suffer In Submarine Tests" *

Well no. The goats don't always die.
Quite a few of them are re-useable.
But not as actual submarine crew
Since they don't have opposable thumbs

And they'd be no use in wartime
Because of smells in confined spaces
Oh and horns getting stuck in hatches
So we use decompression chambers.

Well, they use pigs for testing live ammo
So I suppose we scientists just thought:
"Submarines? Decompression? The Bends?
Gotta be goats. For sure. Absolutely. Yup."

Think about it. One minute I'm at uni.
Then the next I've answered this advert:
"Reckon You've Got What It Takes?
Come And Compress Goats For The Navy."

"Had a hard day at the labs darling?
Any closer to sorting out that pressure problem?
Any fan-mail from grateful sailors then?" Nope.
We sure gave those goat spleens what-for though.

So do the goats get distressed about it?
How should I know? No. I'm not trying to...
Worm out of it. This is what they say:
"They bleat and leap around." Whatever.

No. I don't know what the women scientists think.
But one of the guys got taken off it though.
Oh and Your Brother, the leftie nutter, told me
To have a word with myself. About myself.

What? Didja think we'd put them in their own
Little submarines? With peaked caps?
In an immersion tank. Like in the film
Das Goat? Sorry. Cheap shot. Don't cry.

*Recent headline

Latin Doll

One evening in Ibiza
The dancers took a breather
As Hildegard Von Bingen
Went ambient in the ether

A raver stood there startled
The atmosphere seemed odd:
"What kind of House is this then?"
A nun barked: "House of God."

"For centuries essential
At Evensong and Matin
She chilled a lot of churches
And crucially, in Latin.

Young man, you ought to try it
The liquor, herbs and sound
Till you've been Benedictined —
You haven't been around."

Did Hildegard know singing?
Does cowsmilk come in pints?
Go ask the nuns of Bingen.
(It's ten miles west of Mainz.)

New Riddle For Modern Times

The businessman makes love to me for hours
And drones his long sweet nothings in my ear
I threaten him with breaking up, he cowers
I'd cost him very dear.

Much smaller than my clumsy predecessors
I overpower the quietness of stopped trains
By twittering like electronic birdsong
While microwaving brains.

I know the secret names which lovers whisper
And all the darkened corners where they meet
I hear their fevered pledges and betrayals
And yet remain discreet.

If captured and interrogated later
I won't repeat their bills and coos, not I
If pressed I may divulge a time or number
But not the words or why.

A football ruckus or a city riot
Of course, I cannot start one on my own
But there among the brickbats, masks and poles
I'll grace the battle zone.

My fastest runners fly like unseen pigeons
Who sing their signals, shattering the peace
To sow confusion slipping through the buildings
And past the lines of police.

The farmer loves the harvest that I bring him
The seeds of information which I yield
And broadcasts them to hilltop, house or haybarn
From far out in the field.

Tactless, I'll think nothing of intrusion
Distracting speeding drivers in their cars
My common little voice despised by many
In restaurants and bars.

My subtle shape and smoothness so alluring
A girl may want me...more so than a man,
To hold me firmly during lonely journeys
And use me as she can.

What am I?

A Brief History Of Morse

Dots and dashes didit didit
Did it in the films
And way out in the woolly west
Awaiting freight from Sante Fe,
A marshall in the midday sun
Stands apprehensive with a gun
As sagebrush miles along the track
The buzzards squatting on the poles
Hear signals whisper down the wires
Past cactus, cowskulls, gopher holes
Where tumbleweed goes rolling by.
And three bad hombres wait to die...

Dots and dashes didit didit
Did it down the line
When Mister Morse tapped out his test
"What hath God wrought!"
The sentence stayed
Unanswered by the snoozing past
Until the future spoke at last
And wagons came. And men and mines
Then motor cars and longer lines
Spread out across the yawning land
Till progress had the upper hand.

Dots and dashes didit didit
Did it later on.
In radio blips from storm-tossed ships
Whenever wind and wave kicked up
And hapless vessels in distress
Their flares gone up, gone down, gone out.
Still sent a desperate s.o.s.
The universal rescue shout

The dots and dashes didit didit
Did it for so long
It's odd to think they won't be there
Their crotchet/quavers in the air
Dot dot dot dash — the letter V
The wartime sign for Victory
Was Beethoven's Fifth Symphony
And Samuel Morse's rhapsody
The tune still buried where he hid it
Didit didit didit didit.

Naked Gardeners' Question Time

Caution pruning roses on a ladder
As the thorns may prove to be rapacious
Gruesome fates await the naked gardener
Cutting back the Blackthorn and Acacias

Bending down to tend the Rhododendrons
When replacing soil (ericaceous)
Keep allergic under-hangs from contact
With Ranunculi and Primulaceas

Guard against the holly-leafed Mahonia
Certain strains of Sumac and their juices,
Breasts and bottoms brushing on Laburnum,
And the Firethorn grown for screening uses

As for naked naturists with neighbours
In the garden, shed your inhibitions
But with due regard for good relations
Best consider putting up partitions

Rapid-growing conifers, once trendy
May promote the raising of objections
Pergolas, espaliers or panels
Are just three acceptable erections

Artichokes, rewarding in the winter,
Will create a windbreak in the garden
Tips may be at risk from early frostbite
Therefore keep exposed by day to harden

Finally, if nude when spraying or strimming
Goggles, gloves and groin-protector will do,
In the summer, check for damaged rootstock
And watch out for blackspot, rust and mildew.

Hail

A hailstorm hits the terrace
To warn that summer's coming
And rattles on the skylights
A syncopated drumming
As glistening in the gutters
The hailstones fuse together
The Devil's own confetti
At the marriage of the weather.

The Devil You Knew

The Devil packed his binbag
And clearing out his desk,
Said: "Frankly, I'm astonished.
It's almost Kafka-esque
You could say that I'm gutted
They've sacked me in effect
But that's the problem these days
You don't get the respect
The thing that makes me sickest?
This myth they're putting out,
That Evil somehow triumphs
If good men sit about.

That's rubbish, for a starter.
To propagate your gloom
You've got to know your product
— And how to work a room
Locate your market leaders
Like Ignorance and War
Present them to your client-base
But leave them wanting more.
It's often down to finding
The work for idle hands
Old-fashioned single-tasking
Which no-one understands.

The hooves and hairy hindparts,
They're like a uniform.
And red. What does it tell you?
Professional — yet warm.
It reassures the punters
And lets them know I'm real.
The horns, the cloak, the pitchfork.

Cry out: 'Let's do a deal!'
But where's the Devil's work now?
I mean for pity's sake.
There's only wheel clamping
And daily Rikki Lake.
The planting of Leylandii,
The seating plans for planes,
My self-assessment tax forms
And running British trains."

Travels In Boughton Paidfor

Should I don Tattersall checked shirt
multipocketed action trousers and
garden cardigan? Then, with quiet rabidity,
begin snipping the late-summer fronds
of the wisteria from the honey stone
walls of my Boughton Paidfor cottage?

Should I, while nightingales sing in my
garden, peruse my Dyspeptic Reader's
Book of the English Village and sip
wine club Oloroso, as a drunken wasp
rustles the dried-flower display in the trug
under the planished hod in my inglenook?

What of the tartan blanket which my wife
has placed in the utility room to prevent
the Jack Russells, Barnaby and Tancred,
from making the washing machine muddy
with their scritty little paws? What of our
little brass fleurs-de-Lys hall ornaments?

What will become of our quiet traditions?
The Rover idling on Saturday mornings
prior to the weekly shopping trip to Waitrose?
The contented roar of the garden tractor on
Sundays? The reassuring blink of the standby
light on the Intruder Alert under the eaves?

If there were a public phone, a lavatory
or a post office, People might come.
People staring at us while eating ice creams.
Imagining their own plaster donkeys in our
speedwell-splashed gardens. OUR gardens.
And the coaches. Dear God, the coaches.

We must call an emergency meeting.
Mrs. Cosy McTwee, Rtd. Brigadier Mindset
Mr. and Mrs. Barn-Conversion and
the Newmoneys from Dalmation Cottage.
Some of them have been here for so long,
they can remember the villagers moving out.

The Vicar Recruitment Rap

Bap-chik Baba-baba-chik
C. of E. it's the one for me
We're talkin' 3 (feat. Trini-T.)
Your mobile soul-phone
Comes for free.
It's a Friends and Family to...
Big G.

Gimme a V. Now gimme an I.
Add a CAR to the other side
Heaven's gate is a Park'n' Ride
Who d'ya call
when your granny's died?
Vicar.
Say that name with pride

Service time and the bells go clang
It's a happenin' clappenin' kinda thang
From a warm-up prayer in the vestibule
To a chilled-out church
And an ambient Yule
Though the Sno B. Deep.
And the wind B. Krool
The smell of Faith is a cool Kagoul

V. for vespers. I for an Eye.
The sermon's hot.
But the ink ain't dry
For those in peril on the C
You who would A (pilgrim be)
No R.&R. on the Sabbath Day
Can the dude deliver?
YES WAY!

More E. vicar? Not for me
X-cept E-clesiastically
When the work comes in
Gotta make that call
"Yo! Corinthians!
Quit it." Paul.
(p.p. Father, Son
and Ghost)
The Devil's illin'
But he's toast.

Vicar. As God as it gets.

Bic Pentameter's Poetry Relay

With ashtray full, and baccy down to dust,
A cheap Romanian wine long down his neck,
The poet haunts a cold hungover hallway,
And hopes the tardy postman brings his cheque.
Does he muse on noble Greeks or Romans
With whom he feels some slim immortal link?
No. He rushes headlong at the kitchen
Where he hunches, retching at the sink.

Long ago a caveman made a baton.
And haltingly the man began to speak
History and poetry as he held it.
When he'd done, he gave it to a Greek.
Greeks in turn then handed it to Romans.
Romans watched it splintered by a Hun.
Celts and Saxons hardened it in campfires.
Normans pulled it out when it was done.
Chaucer shined it up as he caressed it.
Shakespeare set his diamonds in the grain.
Restoration poets carved graffiti,
Drank its health and passed it on again.
Later poets coated it in opium,
Passed it on through Tennyson and Yeats,
Up it came to Betjeman and Larkin,
Close to where our hero stands and waits.
Having kept the company of beatniks,
Punks and drunks and urchins of the street,
Battered lies the baton in the gutter
Free to any fool who feels the beat.

Now, back to our poet. What's he doing?
He cannot help himself but starts to write:
"I am Bic Pentameter you ingrates.
Take me out and get me drunk tonight.
Sod your writers' workshops and commissions,
Never mind consigning my slim tome
To the corners of your dullest bookshops,
Pour me in a cab and get me home.
After I have chatted up your sisters.
After I have drunk your cabinet dry.
After I have grabbed your dusty memories,
Frenched them back to life and made you cry.
After I have painted in the details.
Brought to mind your lovers, who are dead.
After I have shown you from the window
All the longed-for landscapes in your head.

I am Bic Pentameter, you ingrates.
Now that you've perused my masterpiece
Tie me raving, naked to my chariot
Slap the horse and send me back to Greece."

Beowulf's Return To The Estuary

Historians now think that the Beowulf poem may not be about southern Scandinavia at all but may be an early account of Saxon raids on the Kent coasts in the fifth and sixth centuries.

Thus spoke Beowulf son of Edgetheow:

So the Hwyfe and I and our three scyldren
took the hring hroad. Hwich was a mistaek
Bumper-to-bumper though the Dartfeord Tunnel
Fynally eonding up near Grays. An healfing nightmaer!
The scyldren at each otheres hthroates and the Hwyfe
bewailing the loss of her Hrattner's gold signum
given to her by Hrothgar, eofter the Great Feast
hwen he hyospitalised her brothere Hwayne.

On the hway back to Gyllinghjam, we stopped in
at a Harvestyr — which was packed and then
into a Mead Hall, eofter I dropped off Hwyfe and scyldren.
Three flasks in and a mighty battle started. This was
because of some warriors just off a longship at Chatham.
One of these hwas well eout-of-ordur, adorned with gold
tattooed around the neck and sheouting the odds.

I mean, there hwas only me, Hygelac The Bald and Welnaf.
Welnaf, fearsome in his Scyell-suit, is a bit naughty in a hruc
and says to this doughnut: "Oi gaezer! Are you calling me
a Cnut?" That hwas it. The hwole thing went pear-scyaped.
Then came this Grendel. Took a Styanley Knife to Hygelac
and gleassed Welnaf in the fyace. In absence of a shootyr,
I took a poolcyu to the beorstard and he hwent down.

Back at Hrothgar's Hall, Hrothgar said: "That won't be the
eond of it, you mark my words." Scyure enuf, two
days later, I'm leaveing the Mead Hall when Daerren says:
"Oi Beowulf, there is a graet fyre in the Carpeork!"
I looked and the Grendel had torched my Feord Escyort.

Eofter that I leoft it. Since Welnaf's brothere put the hword
eout that He hwill deal with The Grendel. But quietly.
And the Hwyfe doesn't hwant my two hyears suspended
being brought up agaen. So that hwas that.

In Memory Of Red U's

(After "In Memory Of Ted Hughes" by Andrew Motion)

Teddy knew and Gunnar knew, but I did not know
and Darren, who was with me, didn't have a clue
how our spun-out last minute miracle double
would be the best ones we'd get. We had been stitched
up before, that I did know, and dribbling from one side
of your mouth the Stella Artois stained your away shirt.

"It's goals did it." you said afterwards, passing one big can
over the punters to me and wiping the froth off the edge,
"You can't have too few goals or you find the whole
shebang goes crash." It was a small front bar
where we were squeezed together jammed in
between the pool table and a large pile of chairs

which was alright if everyone kept still
but wobbled whenever the action went down the
German end. And threatened to fall down altogether
when Basler drove the ball, possibly through Babbel's
legs, inside the far post with Peter Schmeichel still
standing with his mouth open like a fivepenny flytrap

we sat down again, the place so tight in fact
that each of the stacked-up tables now shuddered
every time that anyone so much as lit a fag or pulled
another ring tab. That "goal", drawn out, five-foot screen
in slo-mo was dismal, a low moaning growl broke out
then one or two of the lads had to nip off for a slash

in short they swivelled then fell silent and stared
before the interval and Darren ordered two more Stellas
as well as mine, and went back to his seat chastened.
Ten minutes into the second half, after a lot of pressure
United almost got a goal, Blomqvist steering a deep cross
from Giggsy just over the bar. You dropped your cheese roll,

urging them not to waste time. I might almost have thought
it was over and we were lost to the world then but crucially
we saved it. When Teddy whacked that equaliser into the net
then Solskjaer won it, a game of two corners essentially
the whole bar up in the air, Darren and you kissing each other
the pile of chairs and pints going over, takin' over, Barcelona.

Sir Gawayne And The Green Knight

The Kynge's crewe chilled at Camelot that Krystmas
With many tasty geezeres gotte up in good geare
Blokes with a reppe, well-rayted in a rukke.
People who culde partie with a vengeance.
The do went onne for dayes and dayes.
Arthur's burde mucked-out the place some mornynges
Emptied ashetrays, clered out cacque and cannes.
Hoovered-up the roachez and the rubishe.
Come middaye, it all went raydeo rentals agayne.
For they were as a Millwalle posse, bygge-style
All of themme on Stella biere and shorts
                    all daye.

            Laddes drunkke and stinkeing
            Loades of booze and scoffe
            Everybody thinkkeing
            Somethynge myght go off.

New Yere had hartly hitte home
When Arthur telefonede for a Thai Takeaway
Loude cryed the laddes for more lagere
Arthur shoutede: "Shutte itte. The sprogges are sleepen.
Queene Brenda has gotte the arseayke over this.
She must go to B&Q fyrste thynge for the Sayles.
Sir Gary. See if there's any signe of that scranne yet."
But scarcely had Sir Gary got to garden gayte
When a bigge bastarde on a byke burste inne.
Strayght up the halle, oil on the Axeminstere
Queene Brenda's Ykea lampe lyeing flatte.
No kydingge. This was a honeye-monstre.
Grene leather, grene leggynges, grene skid-lidde
Armes lyke legges. Legges lyke tuggebotes
Bigge bushey beard down to his belte buckle.
                    Strayght uppe

On his bakke a Death's hedde
Manneres very rude
And thenne Sir Gavin said:
"Yow fond of hospital foode?"

The verdant knyght gayve it summe verbal:
"Who's the guv'nor? You bunche of hayre-dressers?"
The Kynge was not beste pleased about this.
And lookked about for backuppe from the laddes.
But nobodye wants a rukke bifore the nosebagge arrives.
You ever tried Thai Takeaway wythe brokken teethe?
"Anybodye want summe?" Asked the Grene Byker.
"I thought you was supposed to be a harde crewe."
You coulde see Arthur was just about to lose itte.
Quietly spoke Sir Gawayne: "Outsyde. Ryghte now."
Arthur said: "No leave itte Wayne." Butte too layte.
This almyghty boundle beganne wythe the berque.
Wayne wellied the wlonke wythe a wheel brayce.
Dogges barkeing. Nayghbour's lyghts come on. The lotte.
Thence came the Fylthe. Blue and twos. Wyth back-uppe.

The Grene Knyght — and full credite to hymme told the Fylthe
Itte was a misonderstandynge. So offe they trotede.
Thenne he turned hym round to Gawayne and sayde:
"You. Returne matche. Yeare's tyme. My turfe. Be there.
          Or else."

Helmet nowe wyth dente
Blood on daygloe veste
Offe the toerag roared.
Somewhere to the weste.

Gawyane slinges his Benne Shermanne in the Zanussi
Breakes open a Beckes and belches lyke a bastarde.

"Thisse is welle bloodie seryious — I'm goner nede a motore."
Kynge Arthur said it would be sortede. Saye nomore.
Wynter dragged onne. Thenne Springe and the F.A. Grail.
Millwalle didn't gette a lookke-in. They was robbede.
So the entyre crewe, Arthur, Sir Gawayne, Sir Daerrenn,
Sir Warrene, Sir Lee, Sir Shaun, Sir Kevinne of New Crosse
And alle the othere Johns flewe to Ibeethere for a fortnyght's funne.
Muche drynkeing, fyghteing and horizontel joggeing was theyre.
Then after, was deportayscheon and some payeing of fynes.
Soone cayme Autumne and thenne soddynge Wynter agayne.
Wayne, hys yere near uppe, must tacqle thysse tossere.
The laddes had a whippe-rounde bifore-hande.
Gawayne was gotte in good ordere by the boyze.
Eighteen-hole Dokke Martynnes, dodgy Mayce gasse
Combatte kecques, welle-sharpenede Stanlye Knyve
Numbere Two croppe, Crombie, Ffforde Cyortina
The cattes knackeres! For he was welle-toolede uppe.
"Put the bastarde oute of businez!" Cryed the Kynge.
"Itte's welle in hande. The quaunte's gotte itte comeing"
                    Calles backe Gawayne.

The trippe to the northewest as bade as it coulde be
Contraflowe, roadwerkes and a smacque-uppe by Stoke
Gawayne, as itte goes endeing uppe neare Northe Wayles
Itte was Krystmas Eve and he was cremecracquered.
By a stroke of lucke, Gawayne mette anothere mayte,
Bertilak, who ranne a garage wyth a nyghtclubbe tacqued onne.
Well-appointede as it happenes. Used to runne wyth Arthur.
What a gaffe! Cocquetayle barre. Faery lyghts. Opticques.
Raisede acrylicque sheepskinne dais, smoked glasse taybil.
Waterebedde. And thysee was just the gueste-bedroome.
"Staye here as longe as you lyke Wayne." said Bertilak.
"I knowe the mushe you're aftere. A ryghte yahoo.

He lives notte two myles from here. Helpe yourselve
Drynkes. Whatevere. My lady, Lynette, will looke aftere you.
Gawayne couldenʼt believe itte and gratefulle, he gaspes:
    "Toppe geezere!"

Krystmas was keppte in a blur of bier and barcardie
Gawayne laye in bedde layte lookeing atte Loadede.
Many a lokke-inne he hadde in Bertilakʼs barre.
Drynkeing. He gotte completeley Schindlereʼs Liste
Thenne three dayes bifore the bigge battle, Bertilak sayed:
"Oute of Bacardie. Iʼve gotte to go to Cashe and Caerrie.
Iʼll be backe layter. Mynde the missus for me."
That mornynge, Lynette came into Gawayneʼs chambere.
A handsome tarte, feisty and fitte-lookeing.
She was tryeing itte onne but Wayne kepede coole.
Whene Bertilak was back, he said: "Awryght thenne?"
"Sweet as." sayes Wayne. "Sweet as."
Bertilak bunges Gawayne a bottele of Bacardie:
"Top manne. Give it summe lewinski thenne."
        Welle goode.

Come the nexte daye, Bertilak drove to Droitwich
To see a manne about the manifolde on his motore.
Same drille. Chille oute dude. Helpen yourselve.
Gawayne was waykened wyth a wette tongue is hys eare.
"Leave itte oute Lynette. Yow are Bertilakʼs beste burde."
By eveninge, Bertilak is backe wyth hys wafty Y-Regge.
"Anythynge happenede lyke?" He lookked atte Lynette.
Gawyane buttonede itte, notte wysheing to saye nuthinne.
Bertilak bunges hym a boxe of Beckes Bier.
        "Sortede thenne."

The thyrde daye, Bertilak beckonnes Gawayne, going:
"I've gotte a little tyckle going offe wyth summe tomfoolery.
Lookke aftere Lynette — there'll be a longe drynke in ite layter."
Gawayne is abed whenne Lynette comes inne.
Fulle beautifulle, hayre falling doune, Wonderebra
Legges withoute ende and some craftie contryvance
Begot from Janetreger, crotchlesse camiknickeres.
Thisse was almost too muche. Gawayne was gaggeing.
But by prayer to St Clintaune, he kept hys wyngknut onne
He beggede one thyng from hys mayte's missus:
Batteryes for his Gaymeboye — flatte since Boxing Daye.
Thys she gives hym and he settles for a snogge.
Wyth no rumtie-tumtie. For thatte was ryght outte.
Thenne Bertilak poppes inne and poures a Pernod.
He gives Gawayne a gold signet rynge for good lucke.
Lynette lowngeing blissed-outte to Teddie Penderegrasse.
"Worde inne your shelle-lyke Wayne. Did she trye itte onne?"
                    "No chaunce."

Nowe dawned the daye of the returne rukke.
Gawayne gotte into geare, wobblie but welle uppe for itte.
A myle up the roade he sees a signe sayeing:
Private Dryve. Keepe Outte. By nowe he's brickyng itte.
The Grene Knyght's garage was huge — a hoogstraaten.
Heareing bangeing from wythinne, he warnes:
"Come over here iffe yow thynk you're harde enough."
"Yow slagge." The Grebo was giveing itte alle of thatte.
"Botteled oute? Yow snowedroppe!" Goes Gawayne.
This was takeing the pysse for the Grene Knyght.
He swunge atte Gawayne's baunce wyth a baysballe batte.
Twyce more he twattede hym. Wayne woulden't go doun.
Whenne Wayne mayced the mushe, itte slowed hym uppe.
But backe he cayme wyth a kicque to Wayne's crickette-sette.

Whych caused Wayne's eyes to welle watere.
"Hadde enough have yow? Hadde enough yow bastarde?"
Gawayne grittede hys teethe: "Do you tayke Swytche?"
                    Theye backked offe.

The Grene Knyght tooke hys helmet off hys heade.
Underneathe itte was Bertilak, Gawayne's hoste.
Gotte uppe lyke a grebo — the fulle maunty.
Gawayne, gobbesmacqued atte being sette uppe
Kicqued atte hys Cyortina doore, swearynge stille.
Bertilak said: "Thyss wasn't doun to me Wayne.
The Kynge had hearde itte said thatte you was alle mouthe.
He wantede to see how you cayme uppe in the washe.
But since you're sounde, we'll call thyss a rezulte."
Wyth thatte, The Grene Knyght slung a canne of Stella
Atte Wayne, who stashed hys Stanleye Knyve awaye.
Thence aftere, theye repayred to Gabriella's
A nearbye knyghtclubbe knowne for lappe-dauncing
Whereupone theye gayve the shortes a severe caneing,
Rezultyng in a rukke wyth seven bounceres
And yette anothere runne-inne wyth the local Bylle.
Bayled outte by Lynette onne Mondaye mornynge
Stille synging: "No-one lykes us. We don'te cayre."
                    As itte goes.

Honi Soit Qui Mal Y Pense.

The Ende.

Old War Stories

Perhaps the ancient films on daytime telly
Drip-feed the small obsession to us still
The little ships, the sirens and the shelters
The "Crikey. Bertie's bought it!" of it all.
The cheery WAAFs with Elstree Studio accents
Who did their bit and waited for the planes
Wore frocks off-duty, stockings, bright red lipstick
Then married men called Charlie, Les or Ron.
Who settled down in semis, flats and prefabs
With furniture marked CC 41
And spawned a brood of adenoidal rockers
Their pimply ingrate sons with red guitars
Who'd learned the war from Hotspur, Combat Library
Victory At Sea and Sergeant Rock.
Wing Commander Gibson, Airfix Spitfires
"Take that, squarehead! Gott in himmel! Aargh!"
Perhaps that's all we had, the jokes and memories.
Like shells ploughed up on farmland, old barbed wire
To compensate for six years requisitioned;
A nationalised Valhalla of our own...

Until the British beat groups toured the bases
And pensioners took boat-trips up the Rhine
And businessmen flew twice a week to Stuttgart
And brickies married nurses from Cologne
And bikers went to Bierfests near to Munich
And ravers went for weekends in Berlin
And councillors to Hamburg on exchange trips
To study housing, transport or design.
And then the thing was over — but it wasn't.
The punchline still remains, without the joke
And hangs there like a catchphrase from a gameshow
Which no-one can remember any more.

Perhaps it's just a tatty family heirloom
A thing kept in a corner in the hall
That's trundled in for birthdays, then forgotten
Reduntant now but ganz gemütlich still
Achtung then Fritz. For you der var is ofer.
The same for us. Although you'd never tell.
The reason we're still laughing is — it's stupid.
And stupid is a thing we do quite well.

Our Part In The Class War

Yer Grandad was a Green Line bus-driver.
Left school at fourteen. Called Gran "the guvnor"
and before he biked off to work at the garridge,
he used to take her a cup of tea up in bed,
Milk bottle on the tea-table, eggs and bacon for breakfast
and gave the plate to the dog to lick.
Came home for his dinner at lunchtime.
Read a good deal and listened to the wireless a lot.

Rented a terraced house for nearly all of his life.
Kept a couple or three beers in the sideboard,
with yer gran's Bristol Cream and his toffees.
Wore a weskitt down the garden Saturdays,
kept a pencil behind his ear and mucked about
in the shed while yer gran peeled the spuds
squinting, a Kensitas hanging from her mouth.

Tin o' salmon, in case o' visitors. Toast'n'dripping
for supper, some Sunday nights. If you brought a
girl home, it was a "cooked tea". Swiss Roll & Evap
for pud. Not sweet. Not dessert. Pud. You didn't
come across garlic, granary bread, sea-salt or
a pepper-mill till you were almost twenty.

The coal cupboard used to be in the kitchen.
An outside toilet. Not loo. Not lav. Never: khazi.
On Monday mornings Gran boiled the hankies
in a special saucepan and threw the lodger's
socks out the top window. He did the front garden
in his shirtsleeves on a Sunday — which had been
a bit controversial in its time. You were amazed
if you went round to a schoolfriend's for tea and
they had a breakfast-room. Or a study. Or a
garden big as Hampshire. And not a long flinty
strip with conker-tree staves for beansticks.

If company came round, the kettle went on and
the telly went off. Occasionally he spat on the fire
and he always pickled his own onions. Weekends
and holidays he let you stay up late. Then he said:
"Come on now Cocker. Clean yer railings, then
up the wooden hills to Bedfordshire." You never
heard him describe himself as working class.
Wasn't the sort of thing he went on about.

The Cycle Path

On a bicycle in winter
Back to Wivenhoe alone
When the smoky Rowhedge rooftops
Through the mist across the Colne
Are forgotten Saxon farmsteads
And the cattle stand like stone
On a still day in December
At the turning of the tide
With the fading roar of traffic
As the Hythe is left behind
For the patterned frosty woodland
Where the leaf-veins in the mud
Are the skeletons of fairies
Delicately strewn around
Then the only living sound
Is the wingbeat of a swan
As it flaps its way upriver
Past the moorhens in the sedge
To a white armada waiting
Silent at the water's edge.

On a bicycle in summer
In the horny pagan heat
Racing with a pleasure steamer
Where the rail and river meet
As a woman on the sun-deck
Sees the cyclist on the path
And she smiles, waving madly
Till he disappears in trees
Where the splinters of the sunlight
Splash the hawthorn leaves with gold
And the hollow-way is dappled
Where the burning ball has rolled

When the winter lost a wicket
After spring came in and bowled
A bluebell haze, the smell of rain
The thunder of the London train
A ship's wash jostles driftwood high
The seagulls see the bikes go by
And shriek along the estuary
To Brightlingsea. To Brightlingsea.

The Grimy Wonders Of The World

The old industrial spectres rattle
Heavy chains on Pennine scars
And groan to be forgiven
By the grey-black grimy hills.
But among those mines and mills
Lay the forge of western wealth
Where the lesions healed slowly
If at all, until by stealth
Time and nature petrified
The iron mastodons and rust,
Rain or ruin dragged the monsters
Down to rubble, shale and dust.

And dirty docks and hulking wharfs
Which witnessed sailing ships come in
Saw holds picked clean by locust cranes
Heard hoists and hawsers creak and keen
While in the country in between
The thrumming ports which burgeoned then
And reeking towns, huge gangs of men
Built long canals which served as veins
To feed their filthy throbbing hearts
Until the coming of the trains.

With Cornish tin, Mancunian cotton
Sheffield steel, and Stafford plates
And everything the British made
The tables of the world were laid.

Now all these towers
And blackened walls
Great edifices leering down
Those bridges built by engineers

Their soot-thick girders linking town
With latticed iron to other town
Will have to do for pyramids
Our Hanging Gardens, Colossi,
A last remaining memory
Of times when giants strode the land
And what we had...
Was industry.

The Ozymandias Clock

*A giant clock which will run for 10,000 years is to be sited in the desert.
It will tick once a day and move its hands once a year, chiming every one
hundred years.*

The first one thousand years or so
Were harder to portray
The clock would move its hands each year
And tick just once a day

It chimed its first millennium
One red and gold-leaf desert dawn
As rusted derricks, armoured cars
And tanks uncovered by the wind
Lay useless, their own monument
To centuries long out of mind

Above the desert, shooting stars
Still littered up the milky way
Rich lovers from a private plane
Took photographs and drank champagne
Made love upon the scorpion sand
Grew old and never came again

Once every twenty years it rained
Then flowers sprang up for a day
And as the sands were washed away
Numberless craft took to the sky
Whose occupants gazed down to see
An ancient caravanserai
Its faded Pepsi Cola sign
And petrol pumps millennia-dry

Later, a psychic railway ran
Disgorging tourists every night
Pale ghosts of men stared at its face
Then glided off in single file
While silent in the moonlight there,
Emaciated desert dogs
Ears down and cringing at the sight
Slunk out into the desert night

The clock still moved its hands each year
And ticked just once a day
The first one thousand years or so
Were harder to portray.

To A Postmistress Upon Retiring

The march of time went past the place
Its staples, pens and paperclips
Dockets, forms in duplicate
Postal orders, stamps and glue
Aged twenty-six she took the shop
Way back in nineteen forty-two
When land girls were her customers.
The airmen, soldiers, farming men
And chaps with different accents
Sent letters home to lonely wives
As warplanes raked the Norfolk skies.

In 'forty-five, the boys came home
'Forty-seven, froze for weeks.
Starving birds tapped window panes
And rationing was still in place.

Through the dreary flooded fifties
Headscarved women, men in caps
Blazing skiffle summers, bees,
Telegrams on motor bikes.
Whitsun weekend, 'sixty-four,
On scooter run to Sheringham,
A lost patrol of London mods
Who puttered slowly past her door.

In all that time and all those years
Of Christmas cards and sisal string
She'd license dogs and wirelesses
Motor cars and t.v. sets
Her weighing scales, arithmetic
And common sense were all she had.

Then half a century on or so
Up comes bold Efficiency
Who won't leave well enough alone
And says she must be 'putered-up.
Hard-disk, screen and god-knows-what
Can't be doing with all that.
Pen and paper did the lot
Wun't be druv. She shut the shop.

The Space Rose

An astronaut
Will bring her home
A whiff of zero gravity
Attar of the Space Rose
A fragrance of the stars.
Rose, how far you've travelled
From Persia, Greece and Rome

And stars which shone
On Roman evenings
On the petals
Of the roses
Floating in Falernian wine
Will cast their light
Again tonight
While weightless
In their chamber
The buds begin to bloom
Outside in the blackness
Silence. Nothing moves.
As fragrance of rosaceae
Pervades her lonely room

And somewhere in the future
The shuttle-lagged commuter
Who's late, let's say
A business trip to Saturn
Buying roses for a partner
Will feel much the same
As any airport traveller
Feels today

Rose, how far you've travelled
From Persia, Greece and Rome
To scent the new
Millennial bazaars
But even to a spaceman
A rose remains a rose,
Though marginally closer
To the stars.

1st Class Honours, University Of Bike-Shed

"A luminous watch strapped round the plums.
The radioactivity neutralises the sperms
And she can't possibly get pregnant. Gospel."

"Get her into a hot bath straight afterwards.
Hot as she can take it. And give her loads of gin."

Robert "did it" with Stephanie. All of us agog
over expressos. "It only goes on for about two
minutes you know," he said, knowledgeably.

A johnny-bag. Belonged to Dave's dead dad.
Washable. Re-usable. Issued in Palestine
When he was in the army. We examined it.
"D'you wanna borrow it then?" Dave asked.

"...a sore about the size of a sixpence,
— on your old chap." Our science master said:
"Then it goes away." An ominous tailing off.

Her four words which punctured the paranoia:
"I came on today." And silence.

"Elastic bands and clingfilm didn't do it. Only fifteen."
Pushing the pram in Pullman Gardens. In school
uniform. Baby started up and he looked panicked.
"Aw nah. Oright then. Where's yore 'kin' rattle?"

The podgy parade of teen mums waddling uphill.
After playgroup. Then later, like tagged prisoners
wheeling their wailing burdens around the co-op.

The kid was never quite right y'know?
She'd jumped off a table loads of times
When she was about three months gone.

"It's sorta gungy." McGuiness was experienced.
"A bit like the inside of your mouth." The four of us
dutifully tested our mouths with our index fingers.

"Yeah I got a little girl back in Gloucester."
Baby-faced labourer homesick for the west,
His lagered-up eyes full of regret.
"I reckon she must be about three by now."

The Shipyard

Bramble, Southernwood and Dock
Unsung among the rubble
Were the salvagemen and saviours
Of a shipyard long in trouble:

"Mr. Bramble," said his colleague
"Since these premises are ours,
Will you formally confirm it
In the trademark of your flowers?
Now the welders won't return here
And the riveters have gone
We must be about our business
As the summer's getting on."

"Mr. Southernwood, the matter
Of this concrete still remains
It may crack with your persistence
And I see you've made some gains
But we fight a losing battle
With the tyrant of the clock
May I venture you prevail upon
The strengths of Mr. Dock?"

"Mr. Dock, you've made some progress
Since removal of the cranes
If the rusty sun assists us
And the heavy summer rains
We could sign the final papers
And conclude this sorry case
Leaving Mr. Moon as watchman
When the winter's on the place."

The Weather Back-cast

Late one winter night,
With the rain lashing down outside,
I woke up with the video tape still running.
The detritus of an evening-in, all around me.
The remote. The full ashtray. The empty bottles.
When suddenly, on the t.v. screen
Was an ancient weather forecast
From some long-forgotten summer
Maybe four or five years earlier.
The weathergirl looked sun-tanned.
She spoke of clear August nights
And how bright the stars would be tonight.
That we could expect some early morning mist
Lingering in certain low-lying areas
Which would soon be burned off by the sun.
She said that it would be another hot day
With a pleasant cooling breeze on the coast.

And I thought of working outside.
And the records playing on the radio then
And walking along the still-warm pavements
To go dusty into a shop.
We knew different people in those days.
I brought my wages home to another kitchen.
The pub was roaring, jukebox blasting
Blokes with money, work — and work to come.
The women, cheerful, tipsy and flirty.
Some brilliant forgotten summer before the split.
And so. Still out-of-it, I go to the front door.
And the rain and the freezing wind desolate me.
And I'll tell you this much:
You never really know what you've got.
Till it's gone.

The Age Of The Train

This is not nostalgia
For the Golden Age of Steam.
Or enhancement of the myth
As such.
Not for blackened arches
Or soot on station walls
Transferred to your clothing
at a touch.

Everything was coal then.
Railways ran on coal.
Even in the Ladies
Waiting Room
Where your mother sat you
By an antiquated grate
Huddled in a brown
linoleum gloom.

This is not nostalgia
For tappets, oil or spanners
The gauges, valves and stopcocks
of it all
The Fag-ash Lils with tea urns
And watery wartime eyes
The gnarly porters smoking
in the hall.

The carnal grunt of engines
Heard somewhere far away
The shower of orange sparks
seen in the night
The hail of red hot gobbets
Spat out beside the track
Which set the gorse embankments
all alight.

No. This is not nostalgia
For how trains used to be
Their racket, their pollution
and their grime.
Their dirty draughty carriages
And sandwiches from hell.
The thing is, that they sometimes
ran on time.

Once Round The Clock

"After you are fifty," said old Johnson,
"Something else goes wrong
With each new year.
Some discoloration, lump or flutter
Tumble, turn or subtle slip of gear
It's the Reaper
Rasping at his workbench
And the sleepless
Copper taste of fear.

Look upon the body as a banger
Doesn't start too easy in the cold
Belches, bucks
And backfires on you daily
Minor troubles with the manifold.
Bumpstart with a brandy
Seems to do it.
Acts like anti-freeze
As you get old.

Eighty years o' motoring, no crashes.
Just some early prangs
Old dancehall fights.
Strictly speaking, needs another service
Engine, chassis,
Steering column, lights.
Not too bad considering I thrashed it
Have to watch the fuel-intake
At nights.

Leakage, that's a problem for the garage.
Ball-joints, they wear out
Of course, your back.

It's a phone-up service
So they tell me
Can't just wander in to see the quack
Everything is 'managed'
Bar appointments.
S'pose it keeps the figures in the black."

Patients should attempt to help the doctor
Don't attend the surgery if ill
Over 65's requiring treatment,
Try to come back later if you will.

Return To Beano Town

By battlements at Bunkerton, the castle
The remnants of an untouched "topping spread"
Since Scrapper, Doubting Thomas and Lord Snooty
Were ambushed by the Gasworks Gang instead
And Bunkerton is falling down
When I return to Beano Town.

The Menace lays in wait for softy Walter
His catty and the shock of hair the same
And after the denouement, still shouts, "Ooyah!"
When punished by his dad in final frame.
A weekly thrashing on the bum
No social workers ever come.

Where Teacher wakes to mortar-boarded bedposts
Cane-patterns on his curtains, teeth in glass
A wife who calls him dear and is his double
Will make him tea and send him to his class
To teach what arid stuff he knows
And leaden-hearted, off he goes

Past Biffo, lateral thinker/style disaster
His weekly catchphrase: "Ah the very thing!"
Who's busy solving problems for a butcher
With giant magnet, fishing rod and string.
The large white fiver which he's won
Not quite enough to buy a gun.

Then back in Bash Street Danny, Plug and Fatty
Will watch resigned, as Smiffy gets it wrong
The Three Bears grow obese on mash and bangers
While Roger dreams up dodges all day long
And Little Plum, your redskin chum
Prefixes every noun with "Um".

Where mums remain at home to do the housework
And dads all have moustaches and a job
Where slipperings and canings come routinely
And slap-up feeds still only cost ten bob
Where order never quite broke down
For long decades in Beano Town.

(Ho ho readers. Now for a feast.)

Round The Counties With Newell

You Worcestershire my Bedfordshire?
You only broke my Hertfordshire
In shanga-langa Lancashire
And la-de-da-de-Derbyshire

A simple breach of Essex here
A flash of pubic Herefordshire
You grabbed me by the Hampshire
Now I'm stuck in missing Lincolnshire

I'm sorry that I Cambridgeshire
Took Cleveland all my senses there
But nothing succeeds like Sussex
I'm so Surrey

I'd come whenever you Cornwall
I must be such a Kent
I've Durham all to death
But the chance was Devon-sent

I bop shoowop Shropshire
Spent three days in de-tOxfordshire
I had a sense of Gloucestershire
But you couldn't care Leicestershire

You told me you would Suffolk-ate
But Warwick you expect from me?
You tied me up in Notts.

You shouldn't pass the Buckinghamshire
You just can't get the Staffordshire
Your bite's worse than your Berkshire
It's not a game of Cheshire

You wouldn't igNorthumbria
Have Merseyside upon me
'Cos a-huh a-huh a-huh a-huh
I think I'm going to Cumbria

Not forgiven Norfolk gotten
Sorry if the ending's rotten
I couldn't in Dorset
How should you be Avon
An occasion like this?

Thanks. But Northants.